THE STRUCTURAL PROBLEM
IN SHAKESPEARE'S
*HENRY THE FOURTH*

# The Structural Problem in
# Shakespeare's *Henry the Fourth*

BY

HAROLD JENKINS

*An inaugural lecture delivered at Westfield
College, University of London on 19 May 1955*

*FOLCROFT LIBRARY EDITIONS / 1973*

**Library of Congress Cataloging in Publication Data**

Jenkins, Harold.
 The structural problem in Shakespeare's Henry the
Fourth.

 Reprint of the 1956 ed. published by Methuen, London.
 1. Shakespeare, William, 1564–1616. King Henry IV.
I. Title.
PR2809.J4  1973          822.3'3               73–4596
ISBN 0–8414–2171–4 (lib. bdg.)          11-26-75

**Manufactured in the United States of America.**

# The Structural Problem in
# Shakespeare's *Henry the Fourth*

BY

## HAROLD JENKINS

*An inaugural lecture delivered at Westfield*
*College, University of London on 19 May 1955*

METHUEN & CO. LTD
36 ESSEX STREET · STRAND · LONDON WC2

*First published in 1956*

CATALOGUE NO. 5878/U

Printed in Great Britain by The Broadwater Press Ltd
Welwyn Garden City, Hertfordshire

# THE STRUCTURAL PROBLEM
## IN SHAKESPEARE'S
### *HENRY THE FOURTH*

෧෪ඏ

IN having the honour to inaugurate a chair of English in this college, I have thought it appropriate to devote my inaugural lecture to the pre-eminent writer in English. A professor of English who gives to Shakespeare such priority of his attention needs, I hope, no defence. But if defence were necessary, I could of course plead the authority of that distinguished body which has honoured me this afternoon by the attendance of so many of its members, the Board of Studies in English, whose collective wisdom has ensured that the syllabus studied in our London school of English gives to Shakespeare a greater prominence than to any other author, not even excepting the author of *Beowulf*. To confine myself to two—or is it indeed only one?—of Shakespeare's masterpieces may be less obviously justifiable. But it cannot be the task of an hour to survey Shakespeare whole, much less Shakespearian criticism. By accepting a restricted scope I must, I am aware, forgo what Dr Johnson called "the grandeur of generality". But whatever may be the poet's business, the scholar and the critic, in their humbler field, before they can come at the grandeur of generality, must be willing to "number the streaks of the tulip". Though they may properly avoid the esoteric, they cannot ignore the particular.

The qualm that I am left with is lest the particular two-headed bloom I have picked for this occasion should not seem the most suitable to present to a women's college. For I am told by one of the most remarkable women in the history of the British theatre that *Henry IV* "is a play which... most women dislike". According to Mrs Inchbald, "many revolting expressions in the comic parts, much boisterous courage in the graver scenes, together with Falstaff's unwieldy person, offend every female auditor; and whilst a facetious Prince of Wales is employed taking purses on the highway, a lady would rather see him stealing hearts at a ball."[1] That, however, was before the emancipation. It would be small compliment to Westfield College if I failed to recognize the great change that has come about since Mrs Inchbald's day. I take this opportunity of paying my respect to the part that Westfield College has taken in the education of women and in the consequent enlargement of women's freedom, which has been so conspicuous a feature of recent social history. A subsidiary aspect of this social change, though one that Constance Maynard can hardly at first have envisaged, is that battlefields and even taverns are now less closed to women than they were. So it is without apology that I cheerfully commend to my students the "infinite entertainment and instruction" that Mrs Inchbald herself admitted might "be obtained from this drama even by the most delicate readers".

The first problem that confronts one in approaching *Henry IV*, and the one about which I propose to be particular, has inevitably introduced itself already. Is it one play or two? Some of you will dismiss this as an academic

[1] Quoted in *1 Henry IV*, New Variorum, ed. Hemingway, p. 395.

question, the sort of thing that only people like professors bother their heads about. Some of you will look askance at it as a metaphysical question, which in a sense it is. But it is also, surely, a practical question: how satisfactorily can either the first part or the second be shown in the theatre without the other? What is gained, or indeed lost, by presenting the two parts, as the Old Vic are doing at the moment, on successive evenings? And thus of course the question becomes a problem of literary criticism. Until it has been answered, how can the dramatic quality of *Henry IV* be fully appreciated, or even defined? Yet the numerous literary critics who have attempted an answer to the question have reached surprisingly opposite conclusions.[1]

Answers began more than two hundred years ago in the *Critical Observations on Shakespeare* by John Upton, a man who deserves our regard for trying to scotch the notion so strangely current in the eighteenth century that "Shakespeare had no learning". Far from accepting that Shakespeare's plays were the happy, or the not so happy, products of untutored nature, Upton maintained that they were constructed according to some principles of art; and his examination of *Henry IV* suggested to him that each of its two parts had, what Aristotle of course demanded, its own beginning, middle, and end. Upton held it to be an injury to Shakespeare even to speak of a first and second *part* and thus conceal the fact that there were here two quite independent plays.[2] To this Dr Johnson retorted that

[1] For particulars of the most important, see the appended Note, which will usually obviate the necessity of further reference in the footnotes to the works listed in it.

[2] *Op. cit.*, 1746. See especially pp. 11, 41–2, 70–1.

3

these two plays, so far from being independent, are "two only because they are too long to be one". They could appear as separate plays, he thought, only to those who looked at them with the "ambition of critical discoveries". In these tart words Johnson shrewdly defined what if not one of the deadly sins, is still a vice and one to which universities are prone. The "ambition of critical discoveries", a natural human vanity unnaturally nourished in our day by the requirements of the Ph.D. thesis and the demand for 'publications', has been responsible for many interpretations of Shakespeare whose merit is in their being new rather than their being true. Yet one must not always accept the accepted. Dr Johnson's contemporaries did not all find it as plain as he did that *Henry IV* was just one continuous composition. It seemed probable to Malone that Part 2 was not even "conceived"[1] until Part 1 had been a roaring success. Capell, on the other hand, thought that both parts were "planned at the same time, and with great judgment".[2]

Among present-day scholars Professor Dover Wilson is on Johnson's side. He insists that the two parts of *Henry IV* are "a single structure" with the "normal dramatic curve" stretched over ten acts instead of five. Professor R. A. Law, however, declares that *Henry IV* is "not a single ten-act play", but two organic units "written with different purposes in view". On the contrary, says Dr Tillyard, "The two parts of the play are a single organism." Part 1 by itself is "patently incomplete". "Each part is a drama complete in itself", says Kittredge flatly.[3] In short, some two cen-

[1] *Shakespeare*, Johnson-Steevens Variorum, 2nd edn., 1778, i. 300.
[2] *Notes and Various Readings to Shakespeare*, [1775], p. 164.
[3] *1 Henry IV*, ed. Kittredge, 1940, p. viii.

turies after Upton and Johnson, scholars are still about equally divided as to whether *Henry IV* was "planned" as "one long drama" or whether the second part was, as they put it, an "unpremeditated sequel". A new professor, his ambition already dwindling at Johnson's warning, might well lapse into melancholy, or even modesty. Modest or not, he can hardly escape the conclusion, reached by another eighteenth-century dignitary in a somewhat different situation, that "much might be said on both sides". Like Sir Roger de Coverley, he "would not give his judgment rashly", yet like the late R. W. Chambers, whose pupil I am proud to have been, he may think that the modesty which forbears to make a judgment is disastrous.[1]

Words like "planned" and "unpremeditated" figure largely in this controversy; and of course they imply intention or the lack of it, and will therefore be suspect in those circles which denounce what is called "the intentional fallacy".[2] I am far from belonging to that school of criticism which holds that an author's own intention is irrelevant to our reading of his work; yet, as Lascelles Abercrombie says, aesthetic criticism must ultimately judge by results: a man's work is evidence of what he did, but you can never be sure what he intended.[3] This position, with the coming of the Freudian psychology, is finally inescapable, but in its extreme form it seems to me unnecessarily

[1] See *Beowulf, an Introduction to the Study of the Poem*, 2nd edn., 1932, p. 390.

[2] This is actually the title of an article by W. K. Wimsatt and M. C. Beardsley in the *Sewanee Review*, LIV (1946), 468 ff., repr. in Wimsatt's *The Verbal Icon*, 1954.

[3] *A Plea for the Liberty of Interpreting*, British Acad. Shakespeare Lecture, 1930, p. 6.

defeatist. When I find *Much Ado About Nothing* beginning with talk of a battle in which those killed are "few of any sort, and none of name", I may infer that Shakespeare intended to write a comedy and not a realistic one at that. But if I wish to play for safety, I may use a phrase of Lascelles Abercrombie's own and speak—not of what Shakespeare intended, but of what he "warned his audience to expect".[1] If we leave aside for the present all question of Shakespeare's intention, what does *Henry IV* itself, as it begins and proceeds along its course, warn us to expect?

The short first scene, filled with reports of wars—wars this time in which multitudes are "butchered"—makes an apt beginning for a history play. But its dialogue announces no main action. Yet certain topics, brought in with apparent casualness, naturally engage our interest. There is talk of two young men who do not yet appear, both called "young Harry", yet apparently unlike. The first of them, Hotspur, is introduced as "gallant", an epithet which is very soon repeated when he is said to have won "a gallant prize". The prisoners he has taken are, we are told, "a conquest for a prince to boast of". Already, before Prince Hal is even named, a contrast is being begun between a man who behaves like a prince though he is not one and another who is in fact a prince but does not act the part. The King makes this explicit. Hotspur, who has gained "an honourable spoil", is "a son who is the theme of honour's tongue", while the King's own son is stained with "riot and dishonour". In the second and third scenes the two Harries in turn appear. First, the Prince, already associated with dishonour, instead of, like Hotspur, taking prisoners in battle,

[1] *Ibid.*, p. 22.

6

plans to engage in highway robbery. Then, when he has arranged to sup next night in a tavern, he is followed on the stage by Hotspur telling how, when he took his prisoners, he was "dry with rage and extreme toil". This practice of juxtaposing characters who exhibit opposite codes of conduct is a common one in Shakespeare's drama. After the "unsavoury similes" that Hal swaps with Falstaff, in which a squalling cat and a stinking ditch are prominent, there is Hotspur's hyperbole about plucking "bright honour from the pale-faced moon". It may not be a classical construction, but there is enough suggestion here of arrangement to justify Upton's claim for Shakespeare's art. We expect that central to the play will be the antithesis between these two young men and the lives they lead. And we shall find that this antithesis precipitates a moral contest which is an important aspect of the historical action of the drama.

The historical action presents Hotspur's rebellion. It is an action which develops with a fine structural proportion throughout Part 1. The act divisions, although they are not Shakespeare's of course, being first found in the Folio, may serve nevertheless as a convenient register of the way the action is disposed. In the first act the rebel plot is hatched, in the second Hotspur prepares to leave home, in the third he joins forces with the other rebel leaders, in the fourth the rebel army is encamped ready to give battle, in the fifth it is defeated and Hotspur is killed. Meantime, along with the military contest between Hotspur and the King, the moral contest between the Prince and Hotspur proceeds with an equally perfect balance. The opposition of honour and riot established in the first act is intensified in the second, where a scene of Hotspur at home preparing for war is set against

7

one of Hal revelling in the tavern. The revelry even in-
cludes a little skit by Hal on Hotspur's conversation with
his wife, which serves not only to adjust our view of Hotspur's honour by subjecting it to ridicule, but also to em-
phasize that the Prince is—with gleeful understatement—
"not yet of Percy's mind". That he is not of Percy's mind
leads the King in the third act to resume his opening plaint:
it is not the Prince but Percy, with his "never-dying
honour", who is fit to be a king's son. At this point the
Prince vows to outshine his rival. He will meet "this gallant Hotspur"—the words echo the opening scene—this
"child of honour", and overcome him. And so, when the
rebels see the Prince in Act 4, he is "gallantly arm'd"—
Hotspur's word is now applied to him—and he vaults upon
his horse "as if an angel dropp'd down from the clouds"—
with a glory, that is, already beyond Hotspur. All that then
remains is that the Prince shall demonstrate his new chi-
valry in action, which of course he does in the fifth act, first
saving his father's life and finally slaying Hotspur in single
combat. Opposed to one another throughout the play,
constantly spoken of together, these two are nevertheless
kept apart till the fifth act, when their first and last encounter completes in the expected manner the pattern of
their rivalry that began in the opening words. The two have
exchanged places. Supremacy in honour has passed from
Hotspur to the Prince, and the wayward hero of the opening ends by exhibiting his true princely nature.

What then is one to make of the view of Professor Dover
Wilson that the Battle of Shrewsbury, in which the Prince
kills Hotspur, is not an adequate conclusion but merely the
"nodal point we expect in a third act"? If we do expect a

"nodal point" in a third act, then *Henry IV* Part 1 will not disappoint us. For there *is* a nodal point, and—I am tempted to say this categorically—it is in the third act of Part 1 that it occurs. In this third act, when the King rebukes his son, the Prince replies, "I will redeem all this . . ."; in the fifth act he fulfils this vow at Shrewsbury, as is signalized by the King's admission that the Prince has "redeem'd" his "lost opinion". Again, in the third act, the Prince swears that he will take from Hotspur "every honour sitting on his helm"; in the fifth act Hotspur is brought to confess that the Prince has won "proud titles" from him.[1] More significantly still, the third act ends with the Prince saying,

*Percy stands on high;*
*And either we or they must lower lie;*

and then the fifth act shows us the spectacle of the hero looking down upon his rival's prostrate form. The curve of the plot could hardly be more firmly or more symmetrically drawn. It does not seem easy to agree with Dr Johnson and Professor Dover Wilson that *Henry IV* Part 1 is only the first half of a play.

If this were all there were to *Henry IV* Part 1, the matter would be simple. But the Prince's conquest of honour is only one aspect of his progress; the other is his break with the companions of his riots. Interwoven with the story of the Prince and Hotspur are the Prince's relations with Falstaff, and these, from Falstaff's first appearance in the second scene of the play, are presented in a way which leads us to expect a similar reversal. The essential thing

[1] The connection here is reinforced by the Prince's use of his earlier image: "all the budding honours on thy crest I'll crop".

9

about Hal is that, scapegrace that he is, he is the future king—the "true prince", the "sweet young prince", the "king's son", the "heir apparent", as Falstaff variously calls him, with whatever degree of mockery, in their first dialogue together. More than that, this dialogue is constantly pointing forward to the moment when he will come to the throne. "When thou art king"—Falstaff uses these words four times in the first seventy lines and yet again before the scene is over. "Shall there be gallows standing in England when thou art king?" "Do not thou, when thou art king, hang a thief." And so on. With these words ringing in our ears, then, we are continually being reminded of what is to come. The words seem, however, to refer to some vague time in the distant future. The Prince's reign will inescapably become reality, but it is at present apprehended as a dream. Falstaff's irrepressible fancy blows up a vast gaily-coloured bubble, and as Bradley recognized,[1] it is because this bubble encloses the dreams of all of us that we feel for Falstaff so much affection. In our dreams we all do exactly as we like, and the date of their realization is to be when Hal is king. Then, everything will be changed—except of course ourselves. *We* shall go on as before, our friend Falstaff will continue his nocturnal depredations, but highwaymen will not be regarded as thieves and punishments will be abolished. Unfortunately, in the real world outside the bubble, it is not the law but we ourselves that should change, as Falstaff recognizes when he says, "I must give over this life, and I will give it over. . . I'll be damned for never a king's son in Christendom." The joke of this is that

[1] 'The Rejection of Falstaff', *Oxford Lectures on Poetry*, 1909, pp. 262–3.

we know that Falstaff will never give over, nor means to; but the joke does not quite conceal the seriousness of the alternatives—give over or be damned; and the idea of damnation continues to dance before us, now and later, in further jests about Falstaff's selling his soul to the devil, wishing to repent, and having to "give the devil his due". What Falstaff's eventual doom is to be could be discerned more than dimly by a mind that came to this play unfurnished by literature or folk-lore. And none of us is quite as innocent as that. We cannot help being aware of an archetypal situation in which a man dallies with a diabolical tempter whom he either renounces or is destroyed by; and to the first audience of *Henry IV* this situation was already familiar in a long line of Christian plays, in some of which man's succumbing to temptation was symbolized in his selling his soul to the devil and being carried off to Hell. It is because it is so familiar that it is readily accepted as matter for jesting, while the jests give a hint of Falstaff's role in the play. I merely pick out one or two threads in the very complex fabric of the dialogue: you will be good enough, I trust, to believe that, in spite of some dubious precedents in the recent criticism of other plays, I am not seeking to interpret *Henry IV* as an allegory of sin and damnation. Falstaff is not a type-figure, though within his vast person several types are contained. And one of them is a sinner and provokes many piquant allusions to the typical fate of sinners, whether on the earthly gallows or in the infernal fire. There is also an ambiguity, to use the modern jargon, which permits Falstaff to be not only the sinner but the tempter as well. The jokes of a later scene will call him indeed a devil who haunts the Prince, a "reverend vice",

11

an "old white-bearded Satan". What I think the play makes clear from the beginning is that neither as sinner nor as tempter will Falstaff come to triumph. Even as we share his dream of what will happen when Hal is king, we confidently await the bursting of his bubble.

To strengthen our expectation even further is what we know of history, or at least of that traditional world where the territories of history and legend have no clear boundaries. The peculiarity of the history play is that while pursuing its dramatic ends, it must also obey history and steer a course reasonably close to an already known pattern of events. The story of Prince Hal was perfectly familiar to the Elizabethan audience before the play began, and it was the story of a prince who had a madcap youth, including at least one escapade of highway robbery, and then, on succeeding to the throne, banished his riotous companions from court and became the most valorous king England had ever had. Not only was this story vouched for in the chronicles, but it had already found its way on to the stage, as an extant play, *The Famous Victories of Henry the Fifth*, bears witness, in however garbled a text. It is hardly open to *our* play, then, to depart from the accepted pattern, in which the banishment of the tavern friends is an essential feature. Moreover, that they are to be banished the Prince himself assures us at the end of his first scene with Poins and Falstaff in that soliloquy which generations of critics have made notorious.

> *I know you all, and will awhile uphold*
> *The unyoked humour of your idleness.*

The word "awhile" plants its threat of a different time to

come when a "humour" now "unyoked" will be brought under restraint. The soliloquy tells us as plain as any prologue what the end of the play is to be.

Yet although *Henry IV* Part 1 thus from its first act directs our interest to the time when Hal will be king, it is not of course until the last act of Part 2 that Pistol comes to announce, "Sir John, thy tender lambkin now is king." It is not until the last act of Part 2 that the Prince is able to institute the new régime which makes mock of Falstaff's dream-world. And it is not of course till the final scene of all that the newly crowned king makes his ceremonial entrance and pronounces the words that have threatened since he and Falstaff first were shown together. "I banish thee." To all that has been said about the rejection of Falstaff I propose to add very little. The chief of those who objected to it, Bradley himself, recognized the necessity of it while complaining of how it was done. Granted that the new king had to drop his former friend, might he not have spared him the sermon and parted from him in private?[1] Yet Professor Dover Wilson is surely right to maintain that the public utterance is the essential thing.[2] From the first, as I have shown, interest is concentrated on the prince as the future sovereign and Falstaff builds hopes on the nature of his rule. Their separation, when it comes, is not then a reluctant parting between friends, but a royal decree promulgated with due solemnity. This is also the perfect moment for it, when the crown that has hovered over the hero from the beginning is seen, a striking symbol in the theatre, fixed firmly on his head. The first words of the

[1] *Ibid.*, p. 253.
[2] *The Fortunes of Falstaff*, pp. 120–1.

rejection speech elevate him still further—"I know thee not"—for the scriptural overtones here[1] make the speaker more than a king. The situation presents many aspects, but one of them shows the tempter vanquished and another the sinner cast into outer darkness. In either case the devil, we may say, gets his due.

The last act of Part 2 thus works out a design which is begun in the first act of Part 1. How then can we agree with Kittredge that each part is a complete play? Such a pronouncement fits the text no better than the opposite view of Johnson and Dover Wilson that Part 1, though it ends in Hotspur's death and the Prince's glory, is yet only the first half of a play. If it were a question of what Shakespeare intended in the matter, the evidence provided by what he wrote would not suggest either that the two parts were planned as a single drama or that Part 2 was an "unpremeditated sequel".

An escape from this dilemma has sometimes been sought in a theory, expounded especially by Professor Dover Wilson and Dr Tillyard, that what *Henry IV* shows is one action with two phases. While the whole drama shows the transformation of the madcap youth into the virtuous ruler, the first part, we are told, deals with the chivalric virtues, the second with the civil. In the first part the hero acquires honour, in the second he establishes justice. But I see no solution of the structural problem here. For though it is left to Part 2 to embody the idea of justice in the upright judge, the interest in justice and law is present from the start. On Falstaff's first appearance in Part 1 he jibes at the law as "old father antic". And he goes further. Included

[1] *Cf.* Luke xiii. 25–7.

14

within his bubble is a vision of his future self not simply as a man freed from "the rusty curb" of the law but as a man who actually administers the law himself. "By the Lord, I'll be a brave judge", he says, making a mistake about his destined office which provokes Hal's retort, "Thou judgest false already." It is in the last act of Part 2 that we have the completion of this motif. Its climax comes when on Hal's accession Falstaff brags, "The laws of England are at my commandment", and its resolution when the true judge sends the false judge off to prison. But it begins, we see, in the first act of Part 1. The Prince's achievement in justice cannot, then, be regarded simply as the second phase of his progress. Certainly he has two contests: in one he outstrips Hotspur, in the other he puts down Falstaff. But these contests are not distributed at the rate of one per part. The plain fact is that in *Henry IV* two actions, each with the Prince as hero, begin together in the first act of Part 1, though one of them ends with the death of Hotspur at the end of Part 1, the other with the banishment of Falstaff at the end of Part 2.

Now, since the Falstaff plot is to take twice as long to complete its course, it might well be expected to develop from the beginning more slowly than the other. Certainly if it is to keep symmetry, it must come later to its turning-point. But is this in fact what we find? Frankly it is not. On the contrary, through the first half of Part 1 the Hotspur plot and the Falstaff plot show every sign of moving towards their crisis together.

Both plots, for example, are presented, though I think both are not usually observed, in the Prince's soliloquy in the first act which I have already quoted as foretelling the

15

banishment of his tavern companions. It is unfortunate that this speech has usually been studied for its bearing on Falstaff's rejection; its emphasis is really elsewhere. It is only the first two lines, with the reference to the "unyoked humour" of the Prince's companions, that allude specifically to them, and what is primarily in question is not what is to happen to the companions but what is to happen to the Prince. In the splendid image which follows of the sun breaking through the clouds we recognize a royal emblem and behold the promise of a radiant king who is to come forth from the "ugly mists" which at present obscure the Prince's real self. Since Falstaff has just been rejoicing at the thought that they "go by the moon . . . and not by Phœbus", it is apparent that his fortunes will decline when the Prince emerges like Phœbus himself. It is equally apparent, or should be, that the brilliant Hotspur will be outshone.[1] There is certainly no clue at this stage that the catastrophes of Hotspur and Falstaff will not be simultaneous.

Our expectation that they will be is indeed encouraged as the two actions now move forward. While Hotspur in pursuit of honour is preparing war, Falstaff displays his cowardice (I use the word advisedly) at Gadshill. While Hotspur rides forth from home on the journey that will take him to his downfall, the exposure of Falstaff's make-believe in the matter of the men in buckram is the fore-shadowing of his. The news of Hotspur's rebellion brings the Falstaffian revels to a climax at the same time as it sum-

[1] *i.e.* This first-act soliloquy looks forward not only to the rejection of Falstaff but also to Vernon's vision of the Prince and his company before Shrewsbury, "gorgeous as the sun at midsummer".

16

mons the Prince to that interview with his father which
will prove, as we have seen, the crisis of his career and the
"nodal point" of the drama. That this interview is to be
dramatically momentous is clear enough in advance: before we come to it, it is twice prefigured by the Prince and
Falstaff in burlesque. But not only do the two mock-
interviews excite our interest in the real one to come; the
mock-interviews are in the story of the Prince and Falstaff
what the real interview is in the story of the Prince and
Hotspur. First, Falstaff, whose dream it is that he may one
day govern England, basks in the makebelieve that he is
king; and then Hal, who, as we have so often been reminded, is presently to be king, performs in masquerade
his future part. The question they discuss is central to the
play: "Shall the son of England prove a thief and take
purses?" Shall he in fact continue to associate with Falstaff? One should notice that although the two actors ex-
change roles, they do not really change sides in this debate.
Whether he acts the part of king or prince, Falstaff takes the
opportunity of pleading for himself. When he is king he
instructs the prince to "keep with" Falstaff; as prince he
begs, "Banish not him thy Harry's company, banish not
him thy Harry's company: banish plump Jack, and banish
all the world." Falstaff's relations to the future king, a
theme of speculation since the opening of the play, now
come to a focus in this repeated word "banish". And when
the Prince replies, "I do, I will", he anticipates in jest the
sentence he is later to pronounce in earnest. If it were never
to be pronounced in earnest, that would rob the masquerade of the dramatic irony from which comes its
bouquet: those who accept Part I as a play complete in

17

itself wrongly surrender their legitimate expectations. In this mock-interview the Prince declares his intentions towards Falstaff just as surely as in his real interview with his father he declares his intentions towards Hotspur. One declaration is a solemn vow, the other a glorious piece of fun, but they are equally prophetic and structurally their function is the same. We now approach the turning-point not of one, but of both dramatic actions. Indeed we miss the core of the play if we do not perceive that the two actions are really the same. The moment at the end of the third act when the Prince goes off to challenge Hotspur is also the moment when he leaves Falstaff's favourite tavern for what we well might think would be evermore. It is at the exit from the tavern that the road to Shrewsbury begins; and all the signposts I see indicate one-way traffic only. There should be no return.

The various dooms of Hotspur and Falstaff are now in sight; and we reasonably expect both dooms to be arrived at in Act 5. What we are not at all prepared for is that one of the two will be deferred till five acts later than the other. The symmetry so beautifully preserved in the story of Hotspur is in Falstaff's case abandoned. Statistics are known to be misleading, and nowhere more so than in literary criticism; but it is not without significance that in *Henry IV* Part 1 Falstaff's speeches in the first two acts number ninety-six and in the last two acts only twenty-five. As for Falstaff's satellites, with the exception of a single perfunctory appearance on the part of Bardolph, the whole galaxy vanishes altogether in the last two acts, only to reappear with some changes in personnel in Part 2. Falstaff, admittedly, goes on without a break, if broken in wind; and his diminished role does show some trace of the expected pattern of development. His going to war on foot while Hal is on horseback marks a separation of these erstwhile companions and a decline in Falstaff's status which was anticipated in jest when his horse was taken from him at Gadshill. When he nevertheless appears at one council of war his sole attempt at a characteristic joke is cut short by the Prince with "Peace, chewet, peace!" A fine touch, this, which contributes to the picture of the Prince's transformation: the boon companion whose jests he has delighted in is now silenced in a word. There is even the shadow of a rejection of Falstaff; over his supposed corpse the Prince speaks words that, for all their affectionate regret, remind us that he has turned his back on "vanity". But these things, however significant, are details, no more than shorthand notes for the degradation of Falstaff that we have so confidently looked for. What it comes to is that after the middle of Part 1 *Henry IV* changes its shape. And that, it seems to me, is the root and cause of the structural problem.

Now that this change of shape has been, I hope I may say, demonstrated from within the play itself, it may at this stage be permissible to venture an opinion about the author's plan. I do not of course mean to imply that *Henry IV*, or indeed any other of Shakespeare's plays, ever had a plan precisely laid down for it in advance. But it has to be supposed that when Shakespeare began a play he had some idea of the general direction it would take, however ready he may have been to modify his idea as art or expediency might suggest. Though this is where I shall be told I pass the bounds of literary criticism into the province of biography or worse, I hold it reasonable to infer from

19

the analysis I have given that in the course of writing *Henry IV* Shakespeare changed his mind. I am compelled to believe that the author himself foresaw, I will even say intended, that pattern which evolves through the early acts of Part 1 and which demands for its completion that the hero's rise to an eminence of valour shall be accompanied, or at least swiftly followed, by the banishment of the riotous friends who hope to profit from his reign. In other words, hard upon the Battle of Shrewsbury there was to come the coronation of the hero as king. This inference from the play is not without support from other evidence. The prince's penitence in the interview with his father in the middle of Part 1 corresponds to an episode which, both in Holinshed and in the play of *The Famous Victories of Henry the Fifth*, is placed only shortly before the old king's death. And still more remarkable is the sequence of events in a poem which has been shown to be one of Shakespeare's sources.[1] At the historical Battle of Shrewsbury the Prince was only sixteen years old, whereas Hotspur was thirty-nine. But in Samuel Daniel's poem, *The Civil Wars*, Hotspur is made "young" and "rash" and encounters a prince of equal age who emerges like a "new-appearing glorious star".[2] It is Daniel, that is to say, who sets in opposition these two splendid youths and so provides the germ from which grows the rivalry of the Prince and Hotspur which is structural to Shakespeare's play. And in view of this resemblance between Daniel and Shakespeare, it is significant that Daniel ignores the ten years that in history

[1] See F. W. Moorman, 'Shakespeare's History Plays and Daniel's "Civile Wars"', *Shakespeare Jahrbuch*, XL (1904), 77–83.
[2] Book III, stanzas 97, 109–10.

20

elapsed between the death of Hotspur and the Prince's accession. Whereas in Holinshed the events of those ten years fill nearly twenty pages, Daniel goes straight from Shrewsbury to the old king's deathbed. This telescoping of events, which confronts the Prince with his kingly responsibilities directly after the slaying of Hotspur, adumbrates the pattern that Shakespeare, as I see it, must have had it in mind to follow out. The progress of a prince was to be presented not in two phases but in a single play of normal length which would show the hero wayward in its first half, pledging reform in the middle, and then in the second half climbing at Shrewsbury the ladder of honour by which, appropriately, he would ascend to the throne.

The exact point at which a new pattern supervenes I should not care to define. But I think the new pattern can be seen emerging during the fourth act. At a corresponding stage the history play of *Richard II* shows the deposition of its king, *Henry V* the victory at Agincourt, even *Henry IV* Part 2 the quelling of its rebellion in Gaultree Forest. By contrast *Henry IV* Part 1, postponing any such decisive action, is content with preparation. While the rebels gather, the Prince is arming and Falstaff recruiting to meet them. Until well into the fifth act ambassadors are going back and forth between the rival camps, and we may even hear a message twice over, once when it is despatched and once when it is delivered. True, this is not undramatic: these scenes achieve a fine animation and suspense as well as the lowlier feat of verisimilitude. But the technique is obviously not one of compression. Any thought of crowding into the two-hour traffic of one play the death of the old king and the coronation of the new has by now been relinquished, and instead the Battle of Shrewsbury is being built up into a grand finale in its own right. In our eagerness to come to this battle and our gratification at the exciting climax it provides, we easily lose sight of our previous expectations. Most of us, I suspect, go from the theatre well satisfied with the improvised conclusion. It is not, of course, that we cease to care about the fate of individuals. On the contrary, the battle succeeds so well because amid the crowded tumult of the fighting it keeps the key figures in due prominence. Clearly showing who is killed, who is rescued, and who shams dead, who slays a valiant foe and who only pretends to, it brings each man to a destiny that we perceive to be appropriate. We merely fail to notice that the destiny is not in every case exactly what was promised. There is no room now in Part 1 to banish Falstaff. A superb comic tact permits him instead the fate of reformation, in fact the alternative of giving over instead of being damned. It is a melancholy fate enough, for it means giving over being Falstaff: we leave him saying that if he is rewarded, he will "leave sack, and live cleanly as a nobleman should do". But since this resolution is conditional and need in any case be believed no more than Falstaff has already taught us to believe him, it has the advantage that it leaves the issue open, which, to judge from the outcry there has always been over the ending of Part 2, is how most people would prefer to have it left. Shakespeare's brilliant improvisation thus provides a dénouement to Part 1 which has proved perfectly acceptable, while it still leaves opportunity for what I hope I may call the original ending, if the dramatist should choose to add a second part. I refrain, however, from assuming that a

22

second part was necessarily planned before Part 1 was acted.

Part 2 itself does not require extended treatment. For whenever it was "planned", it is a consequence of Part 1. Its freedom is limited by the need to present what Part 1 so plainly prepared for and then left out. Falstaff cannot be allowed to escape a second time. His opposition to the law, being now the dominant interest, accordingly shapes the plot; and the law, now bodied forth in the half-legendary figure of the Lord Chief Justice, becomes a formidable person in the drama. The opening encounter between these two, in which Falstaff makes believe not to see or hear his reprover, is symbolic of Falstaff's whole attitude to law— he ignores its existence as long as he can. But the voice which he at first refuses to hear is the voice which will pronounce his final sentence. The theme of the individual versus the law proves so fertile that it readily gives rise to subplots. Justice Shallow, of course, claims his place in the play by virtue of the life that is in him, exuberant in the capers of senility itself. He functions all the same as the Lord Chief Justice's antithesis: he is the foolish justice with whom Falstaff has his way and from whom he wrings the thousand pounds that the wise justice has denied him. Even Shallow's servant Davy has his relation to the law; and his view of law is that though a man may be a knave, if he is my friend and I am the justice's servant, it is hard if the knave cannot win. In this humane sentiment Davy takes on full vitality as a person; but he simultaneously brings us back to confront at a different angle the main moral issue of the play. Is he to control the law or the law him? In fact, shall Falstaff flourish or shall a thief be hanged?

It has sometimes been objected that Falstaff runs away

23

with Part 2. In truth he has to shoulder the burden of it because a dead man and a converted one can give him small assistance. Part 2 has less opportunity for the integrated double action of Part 1. To be sure, it attempts a double action, and has often been observed to be in some respects a close replica of Part 1—"almost a carbon copy", Professor Shaaber says. At exactly the same point in each part, for example, is a little domestic scene where a rebel leader contemplates leaving home, and in each part this is directly followed by the big tavern scene in which revelry rises to a climax. And so on. An article in a recent number of *The Review of English Studies* has even called *Henry IV* a diptych, finding the "parallel presentation of incidents" in the two parts the primary formal feature. I do not wish to deny the aesthetic satisfaction to be got from a recognition of this rhythmic repetition; yet it is only the more superficial pattern that can be thus repeated. With history and Holinshed obliging, rebellion can break out as before; yet the rebellion of Part 2, though it occupies our attention, has no significance, nor can have, for the principal characters of the play. The story of the Prince and Hotspur is over, and the King has only to die.

The one thing about history is that it does not repeat itself. Hotspur, unlike Sherlock Holmes, cannot come back to life. But there are degrees in all things; conversion has not quite the same finality as death. And besides, there is a type of hero whose adventures always can recur. Robin Hood has no sooner plundered one rich man than another comes along. It is the nature of Brer Fox, and indeed of Dr Watson, to be incapable of learning from experience. In folk-lore, that is to say, though not in history, you can be

24

at the same point twice. And it seems as if Prince Hal may be sufficient of a folk-lore hero to be permitted to go again through the cycle of riot and reform. In Part 2 as in Part 1 the King laments his son's unprincely life. Yet this folk-lore hero is also a historical, and what is more to the point, a dramatic personage, and it is not tolerable that the victor of Shrewsbury should do as critics sometimes say he does, relapse into his former wildness and then reform again. The Prince cannot come into Part 2 unreclaimed without destroying the dramatic effect of Part 1. Yet if Part 2 is not to forgo its own dramatic effect, and especially its splendid last-act peripeteia, it requires a prince who is unreclaimed. This is Part 2's dilemma, and the way that it takes out of it is a bold one. When the King on his deathbed exclaims against the Prince's "headstrong riot", he has not forgotten that at Shrewsbury he congratulated the Prince on his redemption. He has not forgotten it for the simple reason that it has never taken place. The only man at court who believes in the Prince's reformation, the Earl of Warwick, believes that it will happen, not that it has happened already. Even as we watch the hero repeating his folk-lore cycle, we are positively instructed that he has not been here before:

> *The tide of blood in me*
> *Hath proudly flow'd in vanity till now.*

In the two parts of *Henry IV* there are not two princely reformations but two versions of a single reformation. And they are mutually exclusive.[1] Though Part 2 frequently

[1] All this is very well exhibited by H. E. Cain (see appended Note). But his conclusion that the two parts therefore have no continuity is invalidated because, like many others, he is content to isolate

recalls and sometimes depends on what has happened in Part 1, it also denies that Part 1 exists. Accordingly the ideal spectator of either part must not cry with Shakespeare's Lucio, "I know what I know." He must sometimes remember what he knows and sometimes be content to forget it. This, however, is a requirement made in some degree by any work of fiction, or as they used to call it, feigning. And the feat is not a difficult one for those accustomed to grant the poet's demand for "that willing suspension of disbelief . . . which constitutes poetic faith".

*Henry IV*, then, is both one play and two. Part 1 begins an action which it finds it has not scope for but which Part 2 rounds off. But with one half of the action already concluded in Part 1, there is danger of a gap in Part 2. To stop the gap Part 2 expands the unfinished story of Falstaff and reduplicates what is already finished in the story of the Prince. The two parts are complementary, they are also independent and even incompatible. What they are, with their various formal anomalies, I suppose them to have become through what Johnson termed "the necessity of exhibition". Though it would be dangerous to dispute Coleridge's view that a work of art must "contain in itself the reason why it is so", that its form must proceed from within,[1] yet even works of art, like other of man's produc-

particular elements in the problem and does not examine it whole. Except when the views of others are being quoted or discussed, the word 'Falstaff' does not occur in his article.

[1] This is a synthesis of several passages in Coleridge. The words in quotation marks are said of whatever can give permanent pleasure; but the context shows Coleridge to be thinking of literary composition. See *Biographia Literaria*, ed. Shawcross, ii. 9. Also relevant are 'On Poesy or Art', *ibid.*, ii. 262; and *Coleridge's Shakespearean Criticism*, ed. T. M. Raysor, i. 223–4.

tions, must submit to the bondage of the finite. Even the unwieldy novels of the Victorians, as recent criticism has been showing, obey the demands of their allotted three volumes of space; and the dramatic masterpieces of any age, no less than inaugural lectures, must acknowledge the dimensions of time. The inaugural lecture has, however, this unique advantage: as its occasion is single, the one thing that can never be required of it is to make good its own deficiencies in a second part.

## NOTE

Of the numerous critical writings on *Henry IV*, I have read most and learnt from many. So although my main thesis about its structure has not, as far as I am aware, been previously put forward, it necessarily incorporates some arguments which have. To my predecessors I gladly acknowledge my indebtedness. It is not least to some of those with whom I disagree—Professor Dover Wilson and Dr Tillyard; from their work on *Henry IV* I have derived much insight and stimulus. The most important discussions of the particular problem are, I think, the following:

Johnson, *Shakespeare*, 1765, iv. 235, 355; C. H. Herford, *Shakespeare*, Eversley edition, 1899, vi. 253–4; C. F. Tucker Brooke, *The Tudor Drama*, 1912, pp. 333–5; R. A. Law, 'Structural Unity in the Two Parts of *Henry the Fourth*', *Studies in Philology*, XXIV (1927), 223 ff.; J. Dover Wilson, *The Fortunes of Falstaff*, 1943, p. 4 and *passim*; E. M. W. Tillyard, *Shakespeare's History Plays*, 1944, pp. 264 ff.; Dover Wilson, *1 Henry IV*, New Cambridge Shakespeare, 1946, pp. vii–xiii; M. A. Shaaber, 'The Unity of *Henry IV*', *Joseph Quincy Adams Memorial Studies*, 1948, pp. 217 ff.; H. E. Cain, 'Further Light on the Relation of *1* and *2 Henry IV*', *Shakespeare Quarterly*, III (1952), 21 ff.; Law, 'Links between Shakespeare's History Plays', *Studies in Philology*, L (1953), 175–82; Tillyard, 'Shakespeare's Historical Cycle: Organism or Compilation?' and Law, 'Shakespeare's Historical Cycle: Rejoinder', *ibid.*, LI (1954), 37–41; G. K. Hunter, '*Henry IV* and the Elizabethan Two-Part Play', *Review of English Studies*, n.s. V (1954), 236 ff.

For further references, see *2 Henry IV*, New Variorum, edited Shaaber, pp. 558–63.